pRAyER BEADS

A POEM CYCLE BY
DON WASHBURN

THE POET'S PRESS
Pittsburgh, PA

This is the 224th publication of
THE POET'S PRESS
2209 Murray Avenue #3
Pittsburgh PA 15217-2338
www.poetspress.org

ISBN 0-922558-83-3

PRAYER BEADS

OLLOW ME.
　I am heading north.
　The pole star beckons.
　The oceans
wash over the bowsprit.
The certain worth
　of an astrolabe
　defines my calculations.
Follow me. I am heading north.

Only by this direction can we plot
a course converging on the inviolable.
Light summons us on our journey. What
we will discover lies behind it All.
Follow me. I am heading north.

I finger my cycling days like prayer beads.
Here is the blessing of the morning shower.
And here I serve my creatures and their needs.
Each of my appointed duties has its hour.
I finger my cycling days like prayer beads.

I take my meals. I read my books. Delights
sometimes arrive like well-known friends. And
when evening comes, I have my bed. These rites
say over and over: amen, amen, amen.
I finger my cycling days like prayer beads.

Imagination is the doorway to heaven,
Take up the book of life. Discover how deity's
manuscripts are illuminated and in
those margins find gorgeous realities.
Imagination is the doorway to heaven.

Make love, then, to what can be. Become
a poet, following God's example. Turn
your mind into a conflagrating kingdom,
where angelic joys consummate and burn.
Imagination is the doorway to heaven.

4

This house has become my monastery.
No women in sight. Whole days go by
without a human voice. Things are sweetly
simple. A single blossom in the window's sky.
This house has become my monastery.

Even cooking becomes a prayer. I proceed
upstairs by Jacob's ladder. The world outside
goes by without a glance. All's here I need.
For the Lord's embassy has come inside.
This house has become my monastery.

COME CLOSER,
    God whispered to me.
  Even in my ignorance I heard.
  Even in the vertigo of my comedy.
  Even in the darkness
    I felt the word.
  Come closer,
    God whispered to me.

As though the postman might unexpectedly
deliver a letter — a lost love writing to me.
One never completely forgotten. And I came to see
someone precious is waiting invisibly.
Come closer, God whispered to me.

I write these tiny poems for your sake.
The smallest match, ablaze, lights up a face.
A modest portion befits a sugary cake.
And what I show you is but a single case.
I write these tiny poems for your sake.

And though they are small and spare you long-
winded gloss and serious scratching of the head,
they are a gift, notes from a half-heard song
that may lift you for a moment from the dead.
I write these tiny poems for your sake.

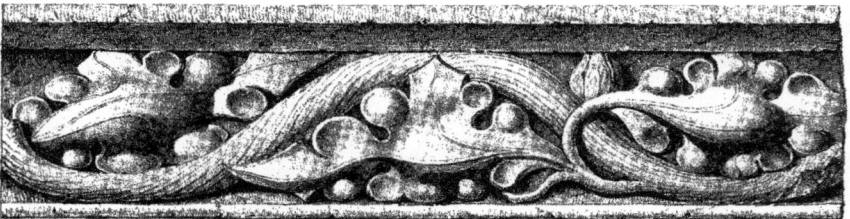

Nothing serves in the end except the truth.
Do not fork your tongue. Do not pretend.
Take stock of everything under your roof.
Pluck out the eye if the eye offend.
Nothing serves in the end except the truth.

The devil is the father of lies. So fill
up your vanity with inner light. Then see
as God sees. Abolish every mirage, until
all that remains is our profundity.
Nothing serves in the end except the truth.

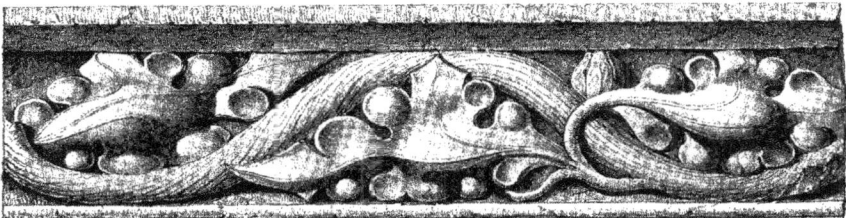

8

This giving that I give you is not mine.
Have you my gift? Well, it's just the wind
passing through my fingers. Or moonshine,
endowing the water where the willows bend.
This giving that I give you is not mine.

For everything is granted. What do I own?
Things that arrive soon pass out of sight.
Generosity is something I have on loan.
There is no debt where there is no right.
This giving that I give you is not mine.

LET YOUR EYES
climb the risen steeple.
The Christ is a bell
calling us to joy.
Towns lie flat, and there are
earthbound people.
Too much grasþing
and rooting can destroy.
Let your eyes climb the risen steeple.

Live with the wind that bloweth where it listeth.
Live with a sky that opens to the stars.
Tell a higher truth with every breath.
Such altitudes and attitudes are ours.
Let your eyes climb the risen steeple.

In this old church how many have sat down
to pray? Their sociable ghosts would fill
the air with murmuring. Hear the sound
of their dutiful hymns, beautiful still.
In this old church how many have sat down?

Ever among them, we shall have a part
in that company. Time cannot numb
the transcendental elections of the heart.
Opening our arms, we bid them welcome.
In this old church how many have sat down?

This is my Father's house, and I am home.
By such a winding path I've found my way.
Who can say just how I came to roam?
And how came back? And with what delay?
This is my Father's house, and I am home.

My heart, it seems, is celebrating Lent.
The Master nods. The Master draws me near.
His touch is better than all argument.
Truths, long forgotten, now are clear.
This is my Father's house, and I am home.

ELIGIONS are like
  those upside-down trees
at the art museum,
  their roots in the sky.
An unsettling alignment.
  Yet priestly decrees
  must take their nourishment
from on high.
Religions are like those upside-down trees.

Each tree subsists in its leafy certitude,
true to its own history. But its starry roots
breathe with the others. And that second sanctitude,
approved in common, lies above disputes.
Religions are like those upside-down trees.

The rose window ignites our metaphors.
More than mandala, more than prayer wheel.
It divides our branching integrity by fours
and in that circumference we live and heal.
The rose window ignites our metaphors.

Orbs confound and delight our eyes
reminding how all things seek their center,
and we ourselves take wholeness for our prize
when we circle our inner sanctums. And enter.
The rose window ignites our metaphors.

The service begins when the candles are lit.
First one. Then a second. Then a third.
Until all of them are blazing, and we sit,
ourselves transfixed by light and strangely altered.
The service begins when the candles are lit.

What is it about this fire that stirs our souls?
We too flicker and grow soft like wax.
We enter then a radiance that enrolls
us, banishing the dark and its effects.
The service begins when the candles are lit.

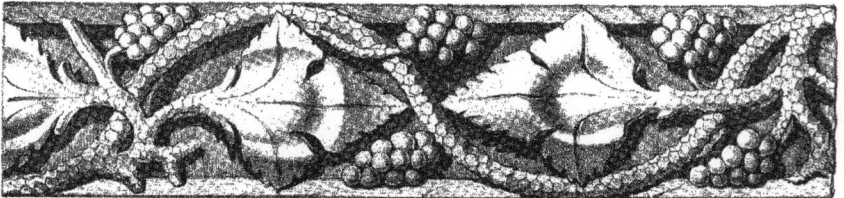

When the choir soars, I soar too.
I lose the anchor that keeps my soul on earth.
Those voices enter me. They make me new,
and I am open to another birth.
When the choir soars, I soar too.

I feel the presence of that company
that holds my guidance and keeps me safe.
They harmonize and hover around me.
I grow thankful as a homeless waif.
When the choir soars, I soar too.

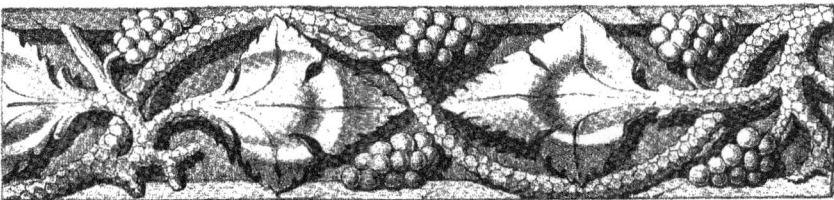

The preacher is the potter. We, the clay.
The strong fingers knead us as we need them.
They hollow us out. That is how we pray.
They fire us up. We are braver then.
The preacher is the potter. We, the clay.

All this to make of us useful flagons,
that we may learn to hold communion wine.
For as we imbibe the sacramental potions,
a well-made vessel can become a shrine.
The preacher is the potter. We, the clay.

HOW CAN WE not love
  our shepherdess?
In whose auspice a sward
  of lambs lies down.
Who drives off the wolves
  of our distress
and leads us all home
  to a safer town.
How can we not love our shepherdess?

The crosses on her splendid robes catch fire
and we are warmed at that communal hearth.
She gives largess and is our sanctifier,
that we be sheltered until another birth.
How can we not love our shepherdess?

No logic nets these fishes — God's decrees.
They swim in paradox. They tack about
in schools together or by finny contraries.
Nor can mind's fishermen haul them out.
No logic nets these fishes — God's decrees.

Who can say was Jesus god or man?
Categories bend and reason hits the roof.
Both bound and free, eternity can span
a tangle of contradictions and be proof.
No logic nets these fishes — God's decrees.

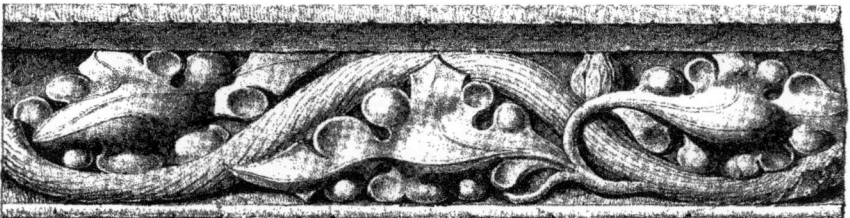

Prayer admits us to the world to come.
Say only the holy name and you are there.
I turn the corner and the morning sun
makes a benediction of the air.
Prayer admits us to the world to come.

It is the talisman that keeps us whole.
It is the meeting place of earth and heaven.
But call aloud from the depths of your soul,
and all that you really need is freely given.
Prayer admits us to the world to come.

White as snowflakes, heads bow in pews.
each a windfall in creations drift,
The weathered effigies bring the news
of flesh grown frostbit, a chilling shrift.
White as snowflakes, heads bow in pews.

But in this winter is the spirit's spring.
where flowers germinate and grow bright.
Behind the ruined masks a promised thing
turns all that perseveres into light.
White as snowflakes, heads bow in pews.

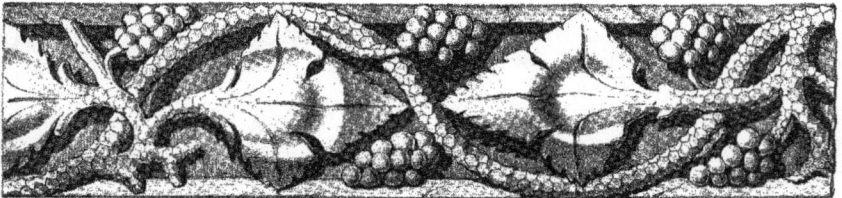

These twelve windows let in a single light.
But further refracted by the fiery glass.
Though histories may multiply in our sight,
we see as one and in one looking-glass.
These twelve windows let in a single light.

Even as our eyes trace the Tiffany panes —
richly stained, icons for the faith,
lost in a rout of colors. Yet also remains
our grand intention, subtle as a wraith.
These twelve windows let in a single light.

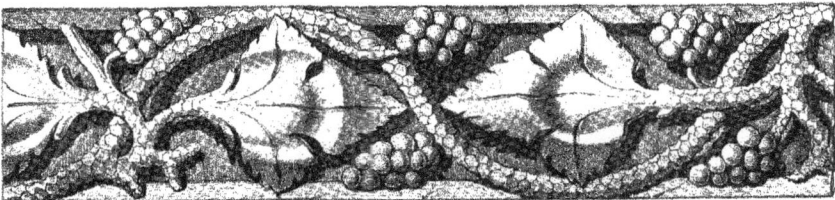

A silent church is like no other silence.
It comes upon you like a morning glory
slowly unfolding its petals. It's an intense
openness where the senses marry.
A silent church is like no other silence.

And at the crown a shimmering borealis.
As though numberless prayers might invest
themselves. And all those kneeling without malice
bathe in that energy and grow blest.
A silent church is like no other silence.

REVELATION GIVES YOU
what you need to know.
It is the operating manual for life.
It is how the avatars
and prophets bestow
divine wisdom. Take their
good advice.
Revelation gives you what you need to know.

So why stumble around in the dark?
Bend an ear to Jesus and to Moses too.
Study your scripture and honor the Ark
of the Covenant between your God and you.
Revelation gives you what you need to know.

Banish reward and the thought of heaven.
Keep no books nor virtue's almanac.
Be an artist without reputation.
Do what you do for its simple sake.
Banish reward and the thought of heaven.

Take up your brush. Use it anywhere.
Make the whole creation slather and shine.
That is your only pleasure and your share.
Life becomes the work of art you sign.
Banish reward and the thought of heaven.

The waters of baptism splash us all,
not just this tiny infant at the font.
More than innocence is needed to forestall
our fall from grace. For that affront,
the waters of baptism splash us all.

There is a Fountain that can soothe our pain
and cleanse us of ancient iniquities,
whose drops fall on us as the gentle rain
and summon up a mercy for every disease.
The waters of baptism splash us all.

This Bible that you read is reading you.
Let scholars quibble and atheists deny.
They cannot gainsay what is always true.
They but expand the speck in their own eye.
This Bible that you read is reading you.

These words are a window to see through,
that greater things may be made exact.
Be humble, then, and receptive too.
Learn a language that is more than fact.
This Bible that you read is reading you.

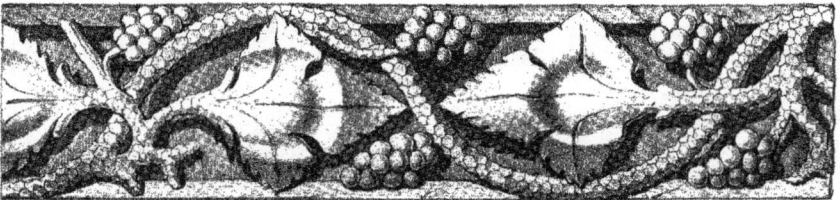

Jesus turned a page in the immortal book.
A new chapter opened. And human kind
recomposed itself. All nature shook.
Our stuttering destinies were redefined.
Jesus turned a page in the immortal book.

Now we may read what we were meant to be.
Now we are edited by the incarnation,
deputized on greatest authority
as collaborators in the unbound creation.
Jesus turned a page in the immortal book.

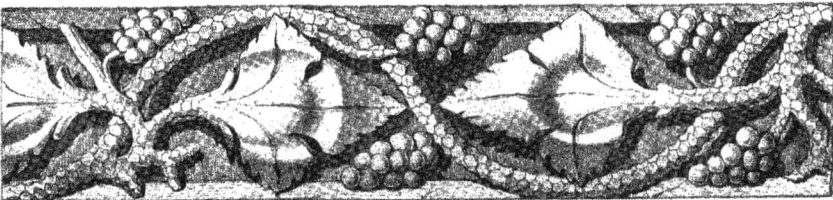

A church too may die or become a remnant.
Pews may empty. And even dutiful hearts.
grow dubious, with good intentions þent.
Faith comes with daylight and in darkness departs.
A church too may die or become a remnant.

Gold, silver, bronze, iron: each age alloys
its predecessor. Know þirit is a seal
we may not break. Shut out the world's noise.
Keep this circle safe where we share our zeal.
A church too may die or become a remnant.

THERE ARE TWO
churches: one outside,
one within.
Attend to both. Your services
are made
to share, so take your place.
Yet sitting in
a pew is not enough. Be shattered and remade.
There are two churches: one outside, one within.

There are no secrets in that inner church.
No Sunday best to hide the breach of trust.
No evasions, but only the humble search
for what the long-suffering Christ has promised.
There are two churches: one outside, one within.

Our communion rebukes the antichrist,
and overthrows the reign of quantity.
All the goods that have been mispriced
are given their rightful worth. Quietly
our communion rebukes the antichrist.

While vanity fair disfigures the TV screen,
and babbles in mindless depravity,
we have a remote to cancel the obscene,
restoring holy silence and charity.
Our communion rebukes the antichrist.

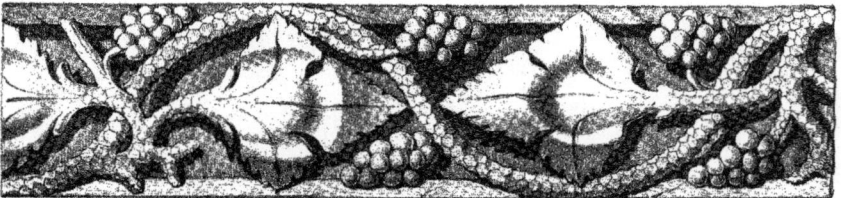

Faith is gold panned by generations.
Not an empty consolation. It's tested
in the creek beds of experience. And once
it shines forth, its truth is never bested.
Faith is gold panned by generations.

Prospectors will tell you where the claim
is waiting. And artful metal smiths will
make of your polished nuggets a golden chain.
Wear it as your evidence. All else is nil.
Faith is gold panned by generations.

Lifting my hands, I feel the currents rise:
electric ecstasies, touching the hem
of God. Fingers alive. Upturned eyes,
A ravishing music. A perpetual amen.
Lifting my hands, I feel the currents rise.

Could that great Presence notice and touch
just for an instant my foolish head, I'd atone
for eons of mindless negligence, such
that legions of light might claim me for their own.
Lifting my hands, I feel the currents rise,

EARTH SHALL HAVE
dominion over man.
This is the greater scripture.
Let us learn
to walk lightly there.
Because if we can
not serve life,
death will have its turn.
Earth shall have dominion over man.

Nature is where heaven comes shining through.
The red men kneel there. They understand.
That day must come when we are kneeling too.
Black Hawk will take Jesus by the hand.
Earth shall have dominion over man.

A vision when the cardinal alights
and flouts his fiery plumage in the bush!
I am another Moses, whose sight ignites,
who tarries like a voyeur in that hush.
A vision when the cardinal alights!

In the church of nature He tells his Homily:
There is a Hand that knows what beauty is.
There is a Healer inviting us to see.
There is a Heaven full of felicities.
A vision when the cardinal alights!

The magnolia tree is blooming. And it is spring.
Another spring and another breath.
A rare patina shines on everything
and for a precious moment cancels death.
The magnolia tree is blooming. And it is spring.

How many more springs will I stop to stare,
finding in the pink blossoms a signature,
and a correspondent, both absent and there,
a love letter from the Prince of Grandeur?
The magnolia tree is blooming. And it is spring.

What is it that this neighborhood cat knows,
who sees me from time to time. "Hello, friend,"
I say to her. The cat bounds to me and goes
over on her back. No need to defend.
What is it that this neighborhood cat knows?

After all, I'm really a stranger. Such trust
could be betrayed. What a compliment.
What a privilege. It makes just
the simple act of petting an event.
What is it that this neighborhood cat knows?

After all these years two things have stayed with me.
A bowl from my mother's kitchen. And the mirror
my father shaved by. When I touch them lovingly
I feel those lost years again: him and her.
After all these years two things have stayed with me.

Some things disappear. Others have a life.
My mother's bowl is still holds my nourishment.
My father's mirror still shows me strife
is only an illusion. It's how the light is bent.
After all these years two things have stayed with me.

At night the train whistle moans along the river,
speaking of lost worlds and bottomless sorrow.
I remember in my childhood bed that same cry,
thoughtless then of yesterday or tomorrow.
At night the train whistle moans along the river.

And now, old and mindful, I hear it again,
and remember those who loved me and passed on.
Those dreaded exits. How can such things happen
as in this listening, they touch me and are gone?
At night the train whistle moans along the river.

OUTSIDE my kitchen window
   the squirrels play,
their tails like bushy rudders
   in the air.
Scrambling on trunks and
   branches, they safely stay
fastened and sure-footed
   everywhere.
Outside my kitchen window the squirrels play.

That endowment speaks to my confidence
in that Power. It summons all life to enjoy
the bounty of aptitude and intelligence.
Such grace! Such agility when they deploy.
Outside my kitchen window the squirrels play.

My neighbor pours chemicals on his weeds.
A piece of the earth strangles. Whatever is
a weed anyway? Just a notion that breeds
arrogance. Nature needs all its presences.
My neighbor pours chemicals on his weeds.

My garden is a tangle. I let things grow.
Maybe I tidy up a bit. But I
pray over living things and leave no
poisons to think about when I die.
My neighbor pours chemicals on his weeds.

Always the buzzing saw-blade of politics.
The radio voices grown jagged with opinion.
Experts pontificating. And the haggling mix
of pundits, making invidious comparison.
Always the buzzing saw-blade of politics.

Whenever a jack-in-the-box expounds, another
pops up to contradict. Neither knows his narrow
confine is an offense against his brother.
The blind stab of claptrap cuts to the marrow.
Always the buzzing saw-blade of politics.

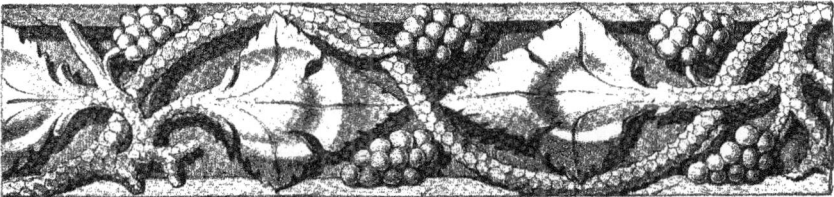

Close down the bar room you call history,
where tarts shimmy, where drunkards brawl.
At the dart board error reigns. And we
step carefully where so many fall.
Close down the bar room you call history.

Should we be laughing or should we complain?
So many have raised fists. So many sink.
So many come together, but with pain.
Let us forswear this degrading drink.
Close down the bar room you call history

Crowds of faces and faces in the crowds.
Stadia packed. Streets filled. Movie credits,
where endless names dissolve. Like living clouds
people float by. You cannot count those droplets.
Crowds of faces and faces in the crowds.

And each a life. Perhaps like yours. Or maybe
an aberration only a god could understand,
who adores the drama of multiplicity,
enrolling you with this wild and wayward band.
Crowds of faces and faces in the crowds.

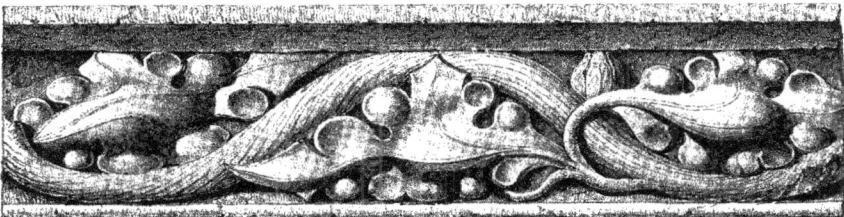

44

FAREWELL, my countrymen.
　　Not much was good.
So many boozers and
　　their childish games.
So many wars. So much
　　innocent blood.
　　The brokers are counting
their ill-gotten gains.
Farewell, my countrymen. Not much was good.

And worse. The desecration of the earth,
who soon will take her cancerous revenge.
Since you measure prosperity by her girth,
your only salvation is the pill, the syringe.
Farewell, my countrymen. Not much was good.

In the casino the slots are dahvening
to Fortuna, goddess of mindless accidents.
She's counterpoint to cosmic justice. The ring
of jingling jackpots obliterates all sense.
In the casino the slots are dahvening.

Worshipping chance eclipses the holy spirit,
the arbiter of worth and wealth. Yet legions
sit at the shuffling tables, their faces lit
by infernal light and vanity's inventions.
In the casino the slots are dahvening.

Is it my face I sometimes glimpse in the street?
There vice and ugliness sit like a troll.
An abomination from which I only retreat,
forgetting the leper whom Jesus made whole.
Is it my face I sometimes glimpse in the street?

Crime smears our features with a satirist's brush
and roiling crowds reek of commonness.
God save me from both the pride and anguish
that turns me away from the worst of us.
Is it my face I sometimes glimpse in the street?

Olympics of the body fall away.
The judges' eyes, grown most particular,
tumble like dice. The gold, the silver may
catch the light, but nature has its calendar.
Olympics of the body fall away.

The ones who fall or stumble are soonest told.
The acrobat slipping off the narrow bar.
In the crowd the also-rans, suddenly old.
Who can keep what time will always mar?
Olympics of the body fall away.

Smack in your Big Mac sits a slaughter house,
stinking of blood, where frightened creatures groan.
Bite into their pain. Slather it in sauce.
Pretend their lives are not precious as your own.
Smack in your Big Mac sits a slaughter house.

Prey if you must and gorge on flesh. But if
all is holy, your crime is sacrilege.
Hope that God will not give you a whiff
of the mountain of corpses that is your sewage.
Smack in your Big Mac sits a slaughter house.

That the rich may have their ornaments,
    a great beast dies.
His flesh is rotting. The predators rip out his tusks.
Dead as a coin, he is covered over with flies.
His majesty dissolves in an endless dusk.
That the rich may have their ornaments,
    a great beast dies.

Wear in shame your bauble of ivory.
Cosmic scales are here confounded. They can't
weigh your mindless pittance of vanity
against the miracle that made an elephant.
That the rich may have their ornaments,
    a great beast dies.

The cheerleaders make their pyramid. They tremble.
Falling is easy. Gravity does not forgive.
Loosen one finger, and it's all a gamble.
A marvelous balance has its negative.
The cheerleaders make their pyramid. They tremble.

You men of science live with this metaphor.
Trifling with nature undoes necessity.
The whole thing may unglue, collapse, before
you stay your hand and learn humility.
The cheerleaders make their pyramid. They tremble.

THE NEWS SAYS
     the world is a disaster.
     Tornados devastate entire towns.
     Babies grow sickly and die
        before their
     lives begin. Deadly cancer
        makes the rounds.
The news says the world is a disaster.

Fanatics explode in the market place,
and thieves deprive people of their savings,
all so we may welcome God's gift of grace
and therein bear the most appalling things.
The news says the world is a disaster.

The TV people hang from invisible strings.
They do their talking with other people's words.
Who is it dangles all these pricey things?
A horde of haggling hucksters and extraverts.
The TV people hang from invisible strings.

The puppeteers are Mammon's doubles. They
buy a face. They buy a ready tongue.
All to keep the registers ringing. That way
the bills are paid and the hash is slung.
The TV people hang from invisible strings.

Your wars exercise the warrior classes.
Wolves have teeth. Tribes their young men.
They can't count coup without their storied clashes?
There is less mischief when they quit your den.
Your wars exercise the warrior classes.

So do not begrudge them their bloody sport.
They keep the barbarians at bay. And when
the body bags are brought home, exhort
the ones still standing to go out again.
Your wars exercise the warrior classes.

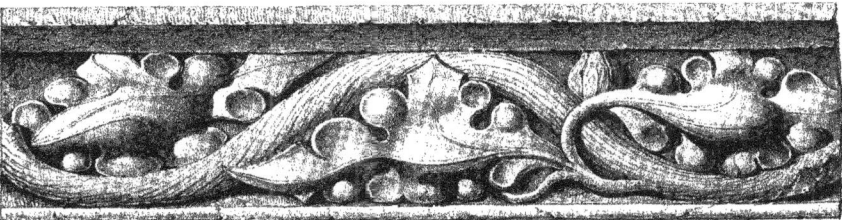

Follow your calling wherever it may lead.
Intentions wilt. But resolve is a golden cross
that will never rust. It must supersede
vicissitude. It must outlast all loss.
Follow your calling wherever it may lead.

Be steadfast in your patience. The marathon
of time will test you. But until life is drained
and destiny is made complete, keep on.
Thus will you win all that can be gained.
Follow your calling wherever it may lead.

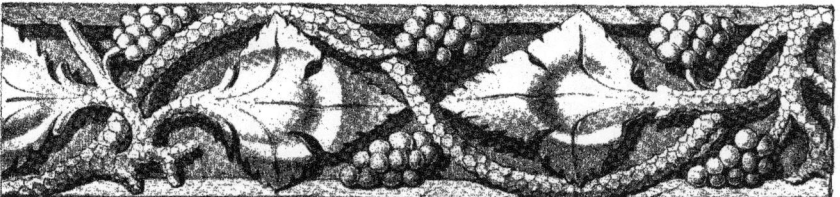

All that is is all that is the One.
A single singularity exists. Everything
else arises and returns. From that sun,
a radiance. Beyond that radiance nothing.
All that is is all that is the One.

This is what we need to understand.
Truth is a fountain of light. At its source
a mystery that shapes this wonderland.
Wherever we look the divine fountain pours.
All that is is all that is the One.

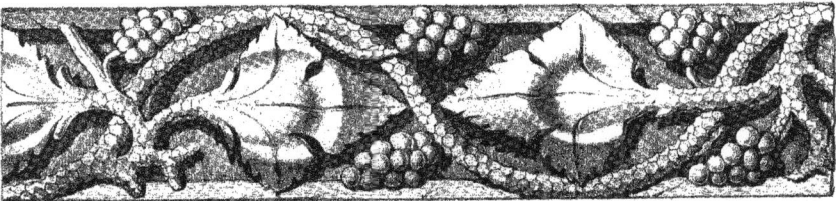

God has in Him all that's thinkable.
Why not a Son? Why not a Holy Spirit?
Why not a lovely Madonna? His mind is full
of miracles. There is no dying to it.
God has in Him all that's thinkable.

So if Lazarus rises from the grave
and Jesus commands the Resurrection,
and blasts the last trumpet, our souls to save,
how ungrateful to refuse the invitation.
God has in Him all that's thinkable.

AVE YOU NOTICED
  that you don't exist,
except as a phantom
  on mind's movie screen?
You are born and die.
  All that can persist
timelessly is the one
and only Being.
Have you noticed that you don't exist?

Cancel this figment and escalate away
to follow perfection wherever it may lead.
Then on that screen a masterpiece will play.
But God only knows how it will proceed.
Have you noticed that you don't exist?

God gave us minds to construe the truth.
How then can it be heresy to think? Yet thought
in love with itself must earn reproof,
if ignorant of what the witnesses have taught.
God gave us minds to construe the truth.

But blind obedience has its hazards too.
We can only reap what we have sown.
Live in the balance. Give guidance its due,
but make the darkest mysteries your own.
God gave us minds to construe the truth.

In the presence of Majesty discretion is best.
Let your prayers be most abstemious.
Do not abuse that audience or request
indulgences beyond your worthiness.
In the presence of Majesty discretion is best.

Remember the feelings from your earliest love,
that mix of timidity and elation.
Be watchful as a sentinel. And, above
all, divest yourself of expectation.
In the presence of Majesty discretion is best.

God is a wind that blows the leaves away,
and with the leaves, all we would not leave:
The hand that holds our own. The sweet play
of words. The haunting music we conceive.
God is a wind that blows the leaves away,

And out the window the garden will not stay.
Nor the cardinal for a moment on the limb.
All will have their winter and gainsay
the greenest summers that we wander in.
God is a wind that blows the leaves away.

We come to this certainty by grace.
As a candle is lit. Or a blind man sees.
Or a smile appears on a solemn face.
It is a quirky quantum without degrees.
We come to this certainty by grace.

Forget exertions. Forget your pieties.
And all the exhortations in your books.
It does not matter how many times you please.
Faith is given as beauties get their looks.
We come to this certainty by grace.

OD EXULTS
in a great profusion.
A googolplex of faces
with no end.
And nearer,
the enormous congregation
of cells where my
five fingers bend.
God exults in a great profusion.

And when I point a finger, a myriad
of shapes swim into view. The world tree
is exploding. So much counting. Who can add
up this riot of specificity?
God exults in a great profusion.

If God is a peacock, a single eye I am.
A single tale in that voluminous tail.
Where all is feathered glory. And beauty's fan
flirts with elucidation and detail.
If God is a peacock, a single eye I am.

So many ways to see. And to be seen.
I have my place in that multiplicity.
Hozanna! should the divine magnificence preen
and find in my sight its own felicity.
If God is a peacock, a single eye I am.

God has ſtamped us with His intelleĉt.
It's an inner light. A ſpark. A holy
ſpirit. A treasure house of guidance. Conneĉt
with this, and you will be human — wholly.
God has ſtamped us with His intelleĉt.

With this gift, this image we come awake.
Greater than angels', our inheritance.
Commanding both heaven and earth, we take
our place as regents, servants of Providence.
God has ſtamped us with His intelleĉt.

There is a god, and there is only one.
The rest are simply idols. Do not bow down.
In that sky there is just a single sun.
Beyond that shining, nothing's to be found.
There is a god, and there is only one.

Nature is a plunging waterfall,
catching the light, but empty in itself.
Cup your hands. Nothing stays at all.
Seek your certainty beyond that gulf.
There is a god, and there is only one.

When God thought me up, I couldn't say no.
Creation's need must surely supersede
dissent. It has an irresistible flow,
a wild wisdom, wherever it must lead.
When God thought me up I couldn't say no.

So I am here and, yes, joyfully so.
for only love could frame my attributes.
And I repay that artistry with all I know.
Hear in these words an affirmation of roots.
When God thought me up I couldn't say no.

Let me be good and celebrate the good,
though cynics rule the world. Auschwitz
has cried out. I will not be shamed should
some human hearts turn black as pitch.
Let me be good and celebrate the good.

More the reason that I refuse cruel
force. My empathy is not a weakness.
It is the precious sign. It is the jewel
that shines behind my fleshly countenance.
Let me be good and celebrate the good.

I have nothing to say about the dark.
Evil happens. Nightmares do come by.
Yes, I've felt some shivers. But even the stark
indignity of death does not terrify.
I have nothing to say about the dark.

Some things are monstrous. But I am ignorant.
I have run too long in the noonday sun.
Rejoicing is my mistress. Others are sent
to chronicle dismay. I'm not the one.
I have nothing to say about the dark.

IN THE POURING RAIN
join where the Sufis dance.
Be part of that exuberance.
Stir and rise.
Turn and whirl. Know
you have entrance
to a cloudburst
from imagination's skies.
In the pouring rain join where the Sufis dance.

Each drop is a gift from that ultimate giver.
So set aside your prudence. And feel the sky
whipping up worlds for your sweet endeavor.
Be soaked in headlong praise before you die.
In the pouring rain join where the Sufis dance.

The Pir has traced a winged-heart on my brow.
Through all the many mansions may it guide me!
The Opener-of-the-Way lives with me now,
and I move fearlessly, with love beside me.
The Pir has traced a winged-heart on my brow.

In that moment I became the gift
and the giver too. What joy to be confirmed
in the soul's election! Now I have only to lift
my eyes. A host of lovers towards me is turned.
The Pir has traced a winged-heart on my brow.

I think of myself as a crumb from Rumi's table.
But even a crumb may hold the flavor. My talk
may stir someone's appetite. If I'm able
to make mouths water, why should I balk?
I think of myself as a crumb from Rumi's table.

This banquet serves all who savor truth.
And if I'm but a condiment, there is the meal.
Eat hearty, my friends. It will surely prove
most nourishing. Your wariness will heal.
I think of myself as a crumb from Rumi's table.

My friend, death will be our referee.
If your atheism is correct and we're done
with God and resurrection, you may smugly
smile in the face of our mutual oblivion.
My friend, death will be our referee.

But if I am right, and that same God exists,
what can I do for love of you but plea
on bended knee: "Lord, here is a list.
of his charities. Grant him clemency"?
My friend, death will be our referee.

In my house a choir of lovebirds sings.
And my whistling cockatiels say, "pretty bird ...
pretty bird ...." All day their chatterings
sanctify me. Their music has become my Word.
In my house a choir of lovebirds sings.

These multi-colored sparks of divinity
chirp in my ears the devotions that they know,
starting a love song of my own to accompany
them. Then I praise God wherever I go.
In my house a choir of lovebirds sings.

I am in love with this English tongue.
the dollops that fell from my parent's lips,
the familiar consonants and vowels wrung
from a thousand years of repartee and quips.
I am in love with this English tongue.

It is like the atmosphere of home, a comfort
beyond translation. And it blazes on the page
of genius, where eloquence holds court,
and words attend the soul's pilgrimage.
I am in love with this English tongue.

MY WAGGING SHELTIES
show what devotion is.
They kiss my hands. They romp.
They leap
to greet me. They tell me when
things are amiss.
When I massage them,
their upturned eyes get deep.
My wagging Shelties show what devotion is.

These furry muzzles have memorized my touch.
They live in my shadow. Or wait for the moment of
my return. What better exemplars to watch
as they teach me the lineaments of love?
My wagging Shelties show what devotion is.

Passing the mirror I glimpse my balding head.
The years, like hair, have fallen out. My face
is no longer my own. Another appears in its stead.
What have I come to? And where is this place?
Passing the mirror I glimpse my balding head.

Must I celebrate all my editions?
This one, I'm sure, is better than demise.
Yet it is not the one I choose for all conditions
or to wear in the afterlife for God's eyes.
Passing the mirror I glimpse my balding head.

There's a mountain of blueberries ready for picking.
Bring your bucket and spend the day. Get down
on your knees. The sky is blue. The thing
you're looking for is bluer still. So round.
There's a mountain of blueberries ready for picking.

Put one in your mouth. Gape at the thousands
in the brambly grass. Do you wonder
what prodigy has planted here? Whose hands
have made such succulence for our plunder?
There's a mountain of blueberries ready for picking.

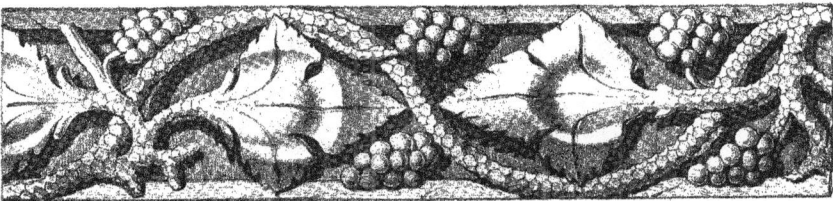

When the angel of death came for my brother,
she came for me. I felt her gentle pull
on my shoulder as I stood at his coffin. Another
might have stiffened, but I grew peaceable
when the angel of death came for my brother.

For I saw she is the dark-eyed sister of love,
smoothing away all suffering and distress.
I imagined my own coffin, where she hovered above,
bending to give me comfort. I felt her kiss
when the angel of death came for my brother.

You will not find greatness here. No matter.
I live this singular life like a million others.
And if in my doggerel I niggle and natter,
be still. I have in myself a million brothers.
You will not find greatness here. No matter.

And who is more fortunate? The one lost
in anonymity, whom liars cannot betray?
Or the icon whose true face is glossed
in a false light, where fantasies play.
You will not find greatness here. No matter.

Think of faith as the science of the heart.
That seismograph beating yes or no,
finding in the flow of things a secret art,
alchemy making us wiser than we know.
Think of faith as the science of the heart.

Experiment, if you will. Do dark deeds
and measure what suffering ensues.
But first discover where that wisdom leads
whose hypothesis determines what we choose.
Think of faith as the science of the heart.

WHEN DIDI wags her tail,
the world wags too.
How can sheepdogs burst
with so much joy?
Is trust ever any sweeter?
My hand's never through
with petting. My heart lives
in her attentive eye.
When Didi wags her tail, the world wags too.

You'd smile if my fancy placed this dog
among the masters who lived for love. Yet she
has taught me a truth without words. No blog
can better say what being itself must be.
When Didi wags her tail, the world wags too.

A pesky sin that's moſt original
lives in my fumbling fingers. I miss the bull's eye
as often as I hit. When good deeds fall
to shreds, I blush. I rush to indemnify
a pesky sin that's moſt original.

The world is always shaking. I pause to lean
againſt the railing. I sit to thread needles.
But accidents crowd my elbow. They careen
regardless of my careful aim. This is
a pesky sin that's moſt original.

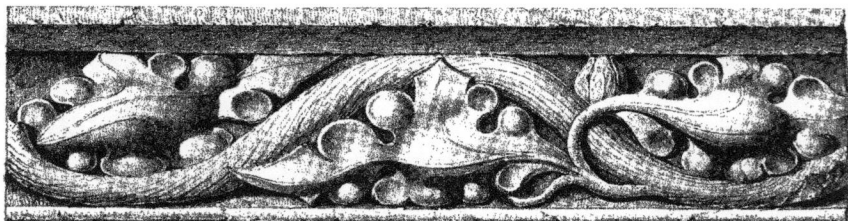

Am I not God's darling, saved endlessly?
Close calls and narrow escapes. The brakes
that put off the accident. The perfidy
evaded or reconsidered. A dozen retakes.
Am I not God's darling, saved endlessly?

And even if I should fail and be reabsorbed
in the finality of things, still I am me.
With more where that came from. Godhead garbed,
I serve the tireless perfection of beauty.
Am I not God's darling, saved endlessly?

An act is like an iron gate that opens,
and once you are in, there is no getting out.
Contingencies nip at you like curs. Though sins
are forgiven, you're clamped in fortune's snout.
An act is like an iron gate that opens.

Since what you settle on meddles in the world
of consequence, pause before that gate.
Consider how intentions may be hurled
into freefall and then become your fate.
An act is like an iron gate that opens.

Beauty lives in the lineaments of woman,
companion not only to sense, but fecundity.
She wraps us in the ribbons of a sun
She drowns us in the funnels of a sea.
Beauty lives in the lineaments of woman.

She is the immortal she, at home
in her lover's arms or in the nursery.
Mysterious presence, come live in my poem.
Plight me your troth and my Madonna be.
Beauty lives in the lineaments of woman.

Before long, I will disappear.
Like a wisp of smoke after the fire is out.
But these few words may have their own career.
Listen while they still whisper or shout.
Before long, I will disappear.

But now I dial your answering machine,
and leave my messages. Listen well.
I have news for you. Some secrets, I mean.
And you are just the person I can tell.
Before long, I will disappear.

87

By now you probably think I think too much,
with all my neat pronouncements.
    While the windy world,
like an unruly flag, refuses such
wrapping up, stays stubbornly unfurled.
By now you probably think I think too much.

Forgive me this flirtation with certainty.
A poet can believe that, yes, wisdom is wisdom!
And syllables can be found that ambitiously,
capture what's otherwise dark or dumb.
By now you probably think I think too much.

CAN YOU HEAR the music
of that brotherhood,
which hand in hand perfects
the slow creation?
Though darker factions
obfuscate the good,
other voices rise,
bringing glorification.
Can you hear the music of that brotherhood?

Be one of them. And if you are able,
dissolve into their plenitude. No company
will better sit at the heart's table
or make friendly the vastness of eternity.
Can you hear the music of that brotherhood?

Children are the ransom that we pay to time.
It is how the flesh remembers us. Yet Saturn
takes them hostage. And if he chooses to dine,
who will deny him? All are devoured in turn.
Children are the ransom that we pay to time.

Yet there are powers greater than appetite.
Those who come are born by pure design.
And, arriving in the spirit to set things right,
discharge all debts, angelic and saturnine.
Children are the ransom that we pay to time.

Do not be hypnotized by pomp and fame.
Yesterday's applause is just an echo now.
What does it matter if they call your name?
A thousand others will rise and take their bow.
Do not be hypnotized by pomp and fame.

"We're number one," the adolescent chants,
a brash narcissus living his own law.
Ignore the blaggards and the sycophants.
Only One matters, and He knows it all.
Do not be hypnotized by pomp and fame.

Emptiness seems to be a half-way house,
neither a prison nor a life. For who
is it that checks in when you espouse
your nothingness? Can you still be you?
Emptiness seems to be a half-way house.

Only a person can celebrate release.
Purge you of yourself, and what is left
if no one lurks in these parentheses
to make amends for this immortal theft?
Emptiness seems to be a half-way house.

Do not dam your tears: Let them flow.
A river finds its certain way to the sea.
The heart must empty to be full. Although
manhood shrinks from sentimentality,
do not dam your tears, Let them flow.

Last night's television uncovered such pain
I wept in my chair without regret. The elves
of sympathy made me feel more sane
and opened me to my other selves.
Do not dam your tears: Let them flow.

Enjoy yourself, but be no slave to pleasure.
Gluttony makes you a gigantic stomach. Drugs
become your master. Things done without measure
will steal your treasure like a band of thugs.
Enjoy yourself, but be no slave to pleasure.

But worst is that disconcerting moment
when your fix no longer fixes and joys are jaded.
Then soullessness becomes your mistress. She's sent
when all the stimulants and highs have faded.
Enjoy yourself, but be no slave to pleasure.

Entertain your demons and be cognizant.
What are they but living energies unchecked?
Their mischievous intentions are spent
in wild improvisations unless they get respect.
Entertain your demons and be cognizant.

Even the devil is himself inevitable,
given that light has need of darkness too.
But keep him in your sight, lest he fool
you with virtues, and your evil is lost to view.
Entertain your demons and be cognizant.

Even the mind may dim and fade to dark.
In the nursing home a friend no longer there.
Only a vague smile. His thoughts embark
without benefit of compass. Words go nowhere.
Even the mind may dim and fade to dark.

What can you say, conversing with the dead?
His sense is absent, and you are absent then.
Yet present to wonder, with recognition fled,
where in the world can he be himself again?
Even the mind may dim and fade to dark.

FOR HUMAN FOLLY,
only a belly laugh!
Since all is forgiven, in all,
myself I see.
The fanatic spouting anathemas.
The daft
millionaire. The pol
and his duplicity.
For human folly, only a belly laugh.

For what is the drift of this comedy?
Together we dodge and feel our way. Your sin
might be my own in another bind. So be
true to the ironies we wander in.
For human folly, only a belly laugh.

Free thinkers are free, but only thinkers.
What good is all this ratiocination
if the heart lies fallow? And the will tinkers
with abominations? The mind's undone.
Free thinkers are free, but only thinkers.

Do not be that diabolical one
trespassing on the sacred. Your ideas
are shadows and must bow to a Sun
whose intellect outshines the galaxies.
Free thinkers are free, but only thinkers.

I have not been generous with my words.
This I confess. And I have not declared
my love enough. Nor praised. Even the birds
exalt the sun. But my lips have not dared.
I have not been generous with my words.

This tight-lipped habit has been my discipline.
Sugar, it seems, might corrupt the pallet.
But here I make amends. If silence is a sin,
loving you all, I labor here to tell it.
I have not been generous with my words.

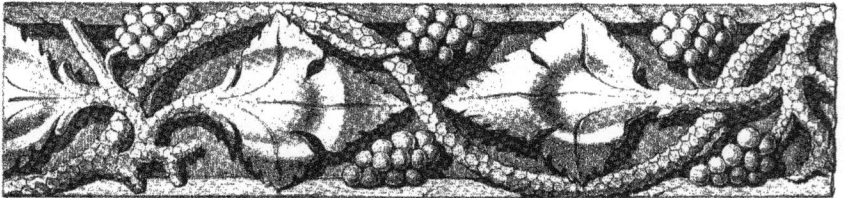

Have conscience, but don't condemn yourself.
There is a latitude that keeps us sane.
Jesus took a burden on himself
so sinners would not shatter under shame.
Have conscience, but don't condemn yourself.

Guilt and blame make unseemly friends.
Pity the wretch who will not forgive or start
the day new. Since God's mercy never ends,
we can always rise again and take heart.
Have conscience, but don't condemn yourself.

I hope you understand that thoughts are real.
They feed on your mind like hungry parasites.
They swell like ticks. They can ravage or heal.
And they commandeer your appetites.
I hope you understand that thoughts are real.

They skulk like devils in your private hell.
They linger in the air when you are gone.
Become your own exorcist and expel
those revenants you cannot rely upon.
I hope you understand that thoughts are real.

If you would become a person, perfect yourself.
Lean into the wind and take your measure.
Would you be human? Then throttle the elf
that holds you prisoner to pride and pleasure.
If you would become a person, perfect yourself.

The tantrums of infancy no longer serve.
Nor the duplicities of youth. Your power
lies in opening to wisdom. Preserve
only the spirit of your finest hour.
If you would become a person, perfect yourself.

I'm not sure I care what people think.
Tens of thousands sat in Hitler's lap.
In the highest truth, the factions find a stink.
Between mind and mind there is a frightening gap.
I'm not sure I care what people think.

Each with his own universe and fate
follows an appointed trajectory.
Do you take exception? Do my ideas grate
on you? Better that both of us be free.
I'm not sure I care what people think.

In the mirror of the soul there is a dance.
Make one bow toward God, he makes seven.
Yet in this stepping he will not advance
without your allemande. What's gained is given.
In the mirror of the soul there is a dance.

Such is the drumbeat of this agency
that only by partnership does it flourish.
By divinest music do we come to be,
and without that same music — we perish.
In the mirror of the soul there is a dance.

In the sum of infinity, I am a single surd.
I'm a divisor from that great dividend.
I am a number pronounced by the primal Word
which continues counting itself without end.
In the sum of infinity, I am a single surd

Yet in that set of all that's possible
I have my special place. For the string
cannot skip me. I'm irreducible.
Together we form a perfect reckoning.
In the sum of infinity, I am a single surd.

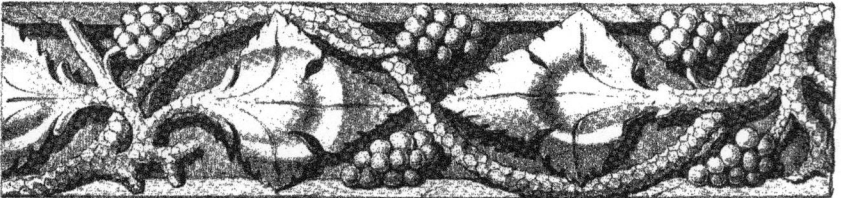

It is not fashionable now to be a believer
in things unseen. The dogmatic priests
of science exorcize whatever will not defer
to measurement. Revelation is deceased.
It is not fashionable now to be a believer.

And see how the flatlanders huddle to deride
those who live on mountains. Their bent
disallows the sacred. And we abide
in their midst as heretics, voices of dissent.
It is not fashionable now to be a believer.

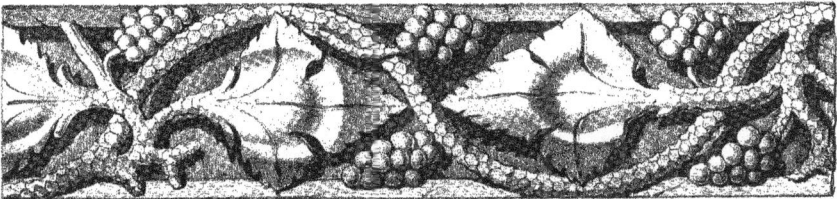

T IS VERY LITTLE
 that you need to know.
Only two things. Harm no one.
And keep in mind
 where the endless flow
of blessings comes from.
 Sing your benison.
It is very little that you need to know.

No diploma is necessary. A dunce
may lead a saintly life. The poorest of
the poor may become a treasure, once
the heart is opened by the key of love.
It is very little that you need to know.

It's what you wish for that entails the sin.
In this way repentance is antidote to harm.
It's the maze of egotism you wander in
that gives your hell its temperature and form.
It's what you wish for that entails the sin.

So empty out agendas, all that's profane.
Take only what is granted and be content.
And if you must desire, desire others' gain
and serve without return Omega's bent.
It's what you wish for that entails the sin.

I've been kept alive to make these lines.
Why else have I been fed? Why given
so many comforts? Why spared the malign
ambush of illness? It's been a kind of heaven.
I've been kept alive to make these lines.

I've been saved to graze in meadows of
language. To what end? To prepare
my thoughts to become an act of love.
To turn my every utterance into prayer.
I've been kept alive to make these lines.

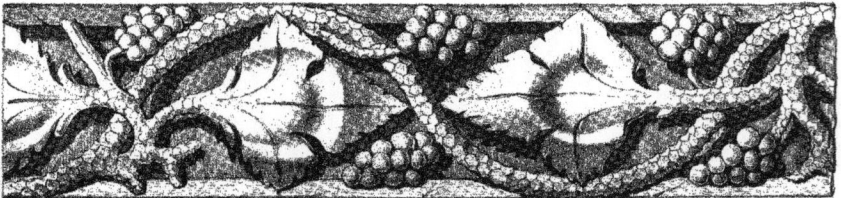

Know the senses for what they really are:
a single station on the dial's band,
in the night sky the pinprick of a star,
at the thundering beach, a grain of sand.
Know the senses for what they really are.

Imagination is another thing.
It makes of a hundred voices a single choir.
At God's lips it gets a secret briefing.
Worlds ignite in that expansive fire.
Know the senses for what they really are.

Let me invite you into my silence, friend,
though these be words and busy as words may be.
There is a place where talking has its end,
opening a window into eternity.
Let me invite you into my silence, friend.

Both of us draw from a single breath,
known without syntax, syllable, or sense,
mysterious as the chaperone we call death,
or the mute embrace of love's magnificence.
Let me invite you into my silence, friend.

Let us not be bedeviled by circumstance.
These ephemera will pass away.
Where is yesterday's failed romance?
Where is the victory that could not stay?
Let us not be bedeviled by circumstance.

You are a surfer on these dizzying tides
The waters churn and threaten to capsize.
But you can fall and you can rise. These rides
are a frolicking sport in eternity's eyes.
Let us not be bedeviled by circumstance.

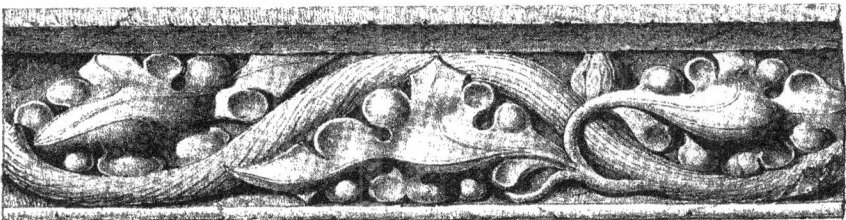

Light takes on the color of the fog.
God must use a kind of baby talk.
His blinding truths would leave us all agog.
Minds shattered, we would only gawk.
Light takes on the color of the fog.

Think of religion as a strange graffiti,
hinting of things beyond our grasp. And yet
the words bring comfort. They hold us sweetly,
as mothers croon when babies are upset.
Light takes on the color of the fog.

We are the music that God listens to.
Our lives are harmonies or discords in His ear.
In that awesome loneliness, forever new,
our alacritous ensembles draw Him near.
We are the music that God listens to.

Performing before that perfect Audience,
we raise our instruments in praise. Make
of us virtue's virtuosos. Let our reverence
be a lovely concertina for His sake.
We are the music that God listens to.

Meaning marries the lesser and the greater.
Take this poem. The lesser is these words.
The greater is what your mind can create or
convert, thoughts migrating here like birds.
Meaning marries the lesser and the greater.

And when great becomes at last the Greatest,
why, the world itself is the lesser. Then we bring
perfection to bear. Then that becomes the test,
transforming us, transforming everything.
Meaning marries the lesser and the greater.

INDLESS PIETY
makes me slightly ill.
Forebear to pucker
and chide like casuists.
Let your light be light.
Empty the till
that is your mouth
of the rant of evangelists.
Mindless piety makes me slightly ill.

And goodness too is cloying, unless you mix
it with surprise. Let merriment circumscribe
your good deeds. And do not mount the crucifix
to wine with Jesus. Better just to imbibe.
Mindless piety makes me slightly ill

Music is the elixir of the heart.
Come! Lift the cup and drink with me.
Be present when the bubbling rhythms start.
Be present to that sweetest harmony.
Music is the elixir of the heart.

This is God's generosity.
Our thirsty ears become a drunkard's quaff,
wherein we find how worlds may come to be
and what it is that makes the angels laugh.
Music is the elixir of the heart.

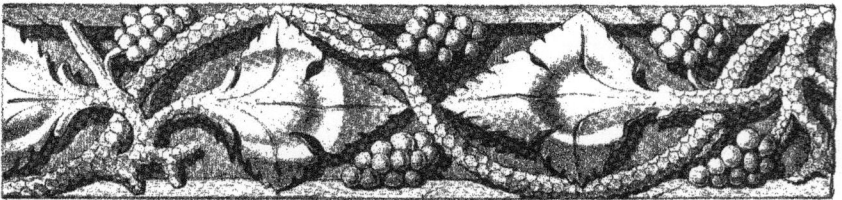

"No one can come to the father save by me,"
Jesus said. For there is knowledge and the act.
Each is heaven's key. Yours by your charity,
and mine by doctrine and a holy compact.
"No one can come to the father save by me."

Welcome, then, all who disdain the words:
the faithless and the heterodox. If love
has kept its vigil in your heart, then towards
the Christ we both go. And will be met above.
"No one can come to the father save by me."

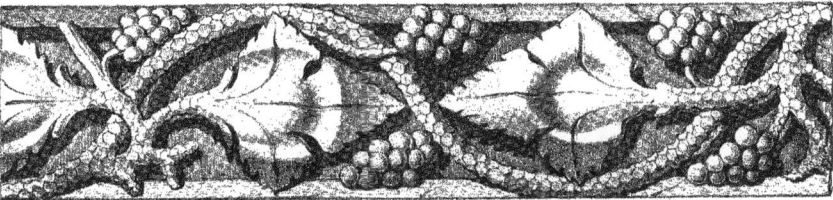

No sense chiding evil doers. They're deaf.
A lump of coal. No mercy. They've run out.
Self-advantage is their only heft.
Their helpfulness is ugly as a pig's snout.
No sense chiding evil doers. They're deaf.

Such is the heart when it hardens. A black
heap. And cold. Words alone will not
suffice. Your most earnest pleading will lack
an ear. Better to lecture an idiot.
No sense chiding evil doers. They're deaf.

Not everybody can fill up with God.
Some lack intelligence, some compassion.
Some were born to turn over sod.
Some compound their emptiness with action.
Not everybody can fill up with God

Since the holy spirit pours in many vessels,
each with its own capacity, no catechism
is final. Another may answer to different laws.
Be generous then with your catholicism.
Not everybody can fill up with God

Nothing can be accomplished without order.
God too thinks in hierarchies.
Fractals are unfolding on every ragged border.
The Necklace of Indra glows with syntheses.
Nothing can be accomplished without order.

And what about the Great Chain of Being,
which binds us all in loops of quality?
Here are the inspirations of the king.
And there the thief and his insobriety.
Nothing can be accomplished without order.

God must bring justice along with love.
Must I not condemn the evil and profane?
And even the heartless monsters who hover above
helpless animals, toying with their pain?
God must bring justice along with love.

If He is only forgiveness, then I will curse
them myself. Do you judge me when I cry
"No!" to those empty eyes. They are not worse
for having felt my outrage before they die.
God must bring justice along with love.

On their beds the lovers lie naked. Do not look!
Some things are forbidden to the eye.
There are privacies that none may brook.
Be blind, or you will be the devil's spy.
On their beds the lovers lie naked. Do not look!

Pornographers hover to command your lust.
But this is a trespass that will corrupt.
Shield your heart. Make innocence your trust.
Medusa watches in wait if you grow rapt.
On their beds the lovers lie naked. Do not look!

O N THIS WORDLY
stage there are no secrets.
Every intention unfolds
and comes to light.
Every act is on display.
Evil gets
noticed. Benevolence
happens in plain sight.
On this worldly stage there are no secrets.

Up in the balcony sit all who ever lived,
applauding the pageant of do and don't. Their
eyes are ever upon us. So do not drift
into duplicity. Be impeccable in that glare.
On this worldly stage there are no secrets.

Once I felt the scald of Sirius,
the whitest light, exploding in my brain.
My thoughts became radiant, delirious
at so much waiting there to make me sane.
Once I felt the scald of Sirius.

I stared into the arc of that dark sky
where Intellect bides, wanting to be known,
and felt with blinding certainty that I
too was light and would never be alone,
once I felt the scald of Sirius.

Only in a living thing can doctrine thrive.
So scotch your screeds and gather in the aisles.
Critics natter and dogmatists contrive.
The only law is how a baby smiles.
Only in a living thing can doctrine thrive.

Popes publish their infallible decrees.
But inspiration like a brush of butterflies
paints the summer day with mysteries.
Embrace your neighbor with a scholar's eyes.
Only in a living thing can doctrine thrive.

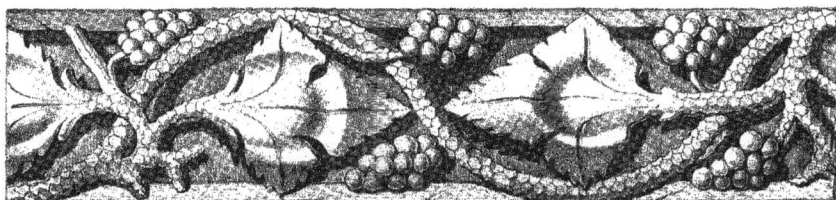

The pain that comes will not be by my hand.
In the torture chamber sadists ply their trade.
May they hear the screams forever and stand
condemned. But I will not be afraid.
The pain that comes will not be by my hand.

Mercy is not an artifact of time.
I make it mine and choose to do no harm.
Then may I weep for those fallen, supine,
crying for relief. I bend and take their arm.
The pain that comes will not be by my hand.

Pardon me if I dodge your compliments.
I've no stomach to fatten on flattery.
I giggle to suppose there is any sense
in words grown obsequious and sugary.
Pardon me if I dodge your compliments.

God only is good the Master's words declare.
And since humility is best in virtue's larder,
appetite must work hard to supper there.
Your rhetoric only makes that work harder.
Pardon me if I dodge your compliments.

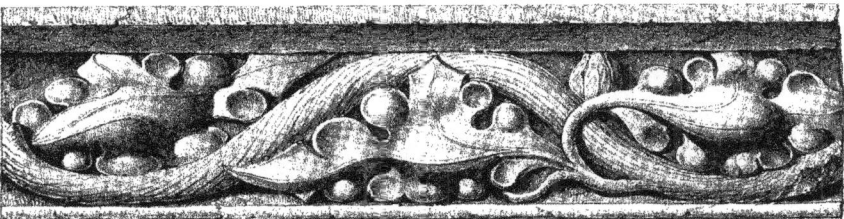

Poems are flowers. They are meant to wither
and vanish. They go wherever voices go
when voices grow mute. Words fail.
Neither mind nor meaning keeps laſt night's
     moon-glow?
Poems are flowers. They are meant to wither.

So pin this poem in your boutonniere,
but know it will be gone like a faithless wife.
And all of us with it. And everything here.
Unless in God's ear it has a second life.
Poems are flowers. They are meant to wither.

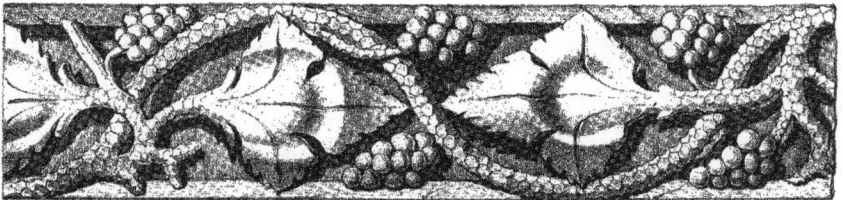

Refuse to be a source of pain or death.
They will come, but never by your hand.
All creatures alive with each passing breath
love their lives as we do. Understand!
Refuse to be a source of pain or death.

Shut down your slaughter houses. Be content
with harmless sustenance. And do not play
the hunter with God's creatures. All are sent
to teach us mercy and beautify our way.
Refuse to be a source of pain or death.

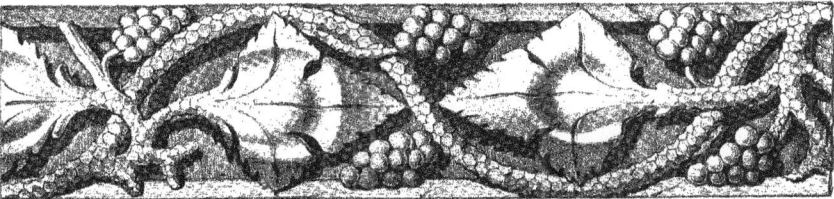

SCHOOL YOUR WILL
 to be mortality's friend.
The world will loosen its grip
 and grow dim.
Detachment mimics
 that most certain end.
So take the poison
to fortify your vim.
School your will to be mortality's friend.

Repudiate your cravings and turn away
They are swiftly gone. Nothing can be kept.
Die before death is what the Sufis say.
Then you are released as if time slept.
School your will to be mortality's friend.

Since love cannot be forced, we are free,
and, being free, may countermand the good.
Easier to sink in ego's catastrophe
than lift with the sun as sunflowers should.
Since love cannot be forced, we are free.

"I will not have a God who is myself,"
a poet said. So what is this freedom worth?
Only to search out perfection's wealth
and mirror the paragon that gave us birth.
Since love cannot be forced, we are free.

So what if I ramble, or I seem to preach.
Ecclesiastes knew a thing or two.
My many years give me a greater reach.
But I once sat in the dark next to you.
So what if I ramble, or I seem to preach.

Like a man, who climbs a mountain and calls back
to those strung out behind him, and for their sake,
warns of dreadful chasms on the track
and foretells what glorious vistas lie in wait,
so what if I ramble, or I seem to preach.

Some call for salvation. Some for union.
If I'm saved, why then I'm still myself.
But if I merge into that limitless One
I am not I; no more I is felt.
Some call for salvation. Some for union.

Perhaps I can choose to cherish what I've been.
God loves my singularity, doesn't He?
Courtesy, then, conserves everything within,
for it is the doorway to my eternity.
Some call for salvation. Some for union.

Some embrace mastery, some charity.
These are the antipodes of politics.
Mastery commands, and new things come to be.
Charity brings sympathy into the mix.
Some embrace mastery, some charity.

Conservatives and liberals look askance
at one another and forget that power
and love must coexist. It is arrogance
to think the root can ripen without the flower.
Some embrace mastery, some charity.

Sometimes, John Donne, you come to mind.
You had conceit enough to live in both the worlds.
Lover and priest, you were never blind
to what the sparkle of imagination unfolds.
Sometimes, John Donne, you come to mind.

For wit undoes the categorical
and fashions a language made to disconcert.
And when a pun grows metaphysical,
God and man express themselves in concert.
Sometimes, John Donne, you come to mind.

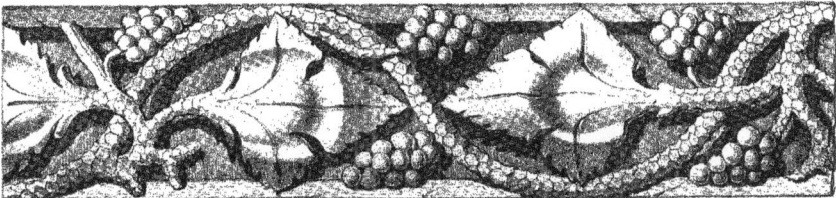

Stop and applaud the ones with special gifts.
They bring perfection into human form.
The miracle of their endowment lifts
us up, and excellence seems the norm.
Stop and applaud the ones with special gifts.

When they come before us, we are apprised
of Providence, that splendor for the taking.
And there is an oracle that sees in their eyes
the greater self that waits upon our waking.
Stop and applaud the ones with special gifts.

Tears for those who have lost the light.
Who have sullied the world and have spilt blood.
whose predatory howl shatters the night,
who have hardened their hearts
     against mercy and good.
Tears for those who have lost the light.

I have seen the faces distorted with hate.
And shuddered. Yet wondered too if some pity
might yet redeem the horror of their fate
and teach them what it is that they must be.
Tears for those who have lost the light.

Thank you, Lord, for the gift of breath.
For the shining garland of my consciousness.
For my body's strength. For the roulette
of day and night. And for all that is ageless.
Thank you, Lord, for the gift of breath.

Out of whatever oblivion I have come,
to awaken in the round of circumstance,
I turn in joy and with impeccable aplomb
accept my invitation to the dance.
Thank you, Lord, for the gift of breath.

THAT PEACE be with you,
   I offer my hand.
I see in your steady eyes
   that we can skirt
formality. And for
a moment stand
linked, feeling
our fellowship in concert.

That peace be with you, I offer my hand.
Your touch reminds me that our apartness
has no part in our persuasion. And peace
settles on this harmony like the quietness
of two swans on a lake, swimming at their ease.
That peace be with you, I offer my hand.

The eye of the heart makes known the Paraclete.
Do not, then, damn up your tears. Let them
polish the secret lens and flood the seat
of wisdom. Bathe in ſpirit. Shine like a gem.
The eye of the heart makes known the Paraclete.

Then will you see beyond the vice of sense,
and by this inner beacon rise to be
a confidant of such magnificence
that all your sightings will be epiphany.
The eye of the heart makes known the Paraclete.

The force be with you. But not only the force.
A person only can take your hand. And what
is a person? You and I are that, of course.
And the Creator no less by whom we are begot.
The force be with you. But not only the force.

Energy itself can do nothing alone.
It is a bare happening, empty of love.
Only a voice, companion to our own,
can open our hearts to all that lies above.
The force be with you. But not only the force.

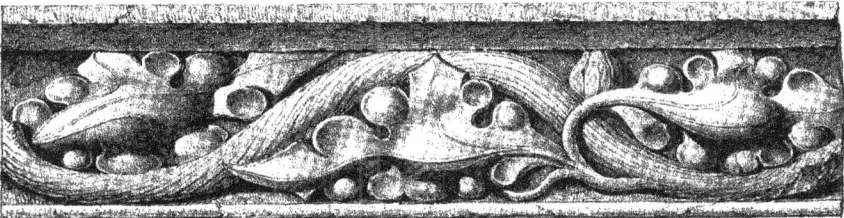

The heart is a cathedral. Come join me there.
This page will crumble, but do not count the cost.
A tower rises in that endless air.
where beauty is kept and cannot be lost.
The heart is a cathedral. Come join me there?

True poems have a life and are sanctified.
Time is helpless. Light remembering
light invites us in. Set modesty aside.
Powers preserve whoever rises to sing.
The heart is a cathedral. Come join me there?

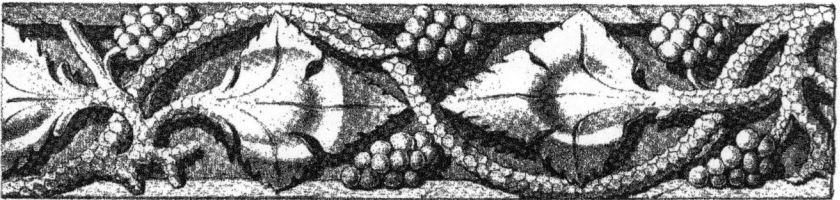

The honey bee of attention brought you here.
And these, my blooms, are inviting you to stay.
Lose yourself among the petals. Take care
to pollinate and bear the sweetness away.
The honey bee of attention brought you here.

Be mindful then and know this garden is yours.
Together we fructify the world. Nothing gained
unless meanings pass between us. Such tours
fill wisdom's hive. Secrets are explained.
The honey bee of attention brought you here.

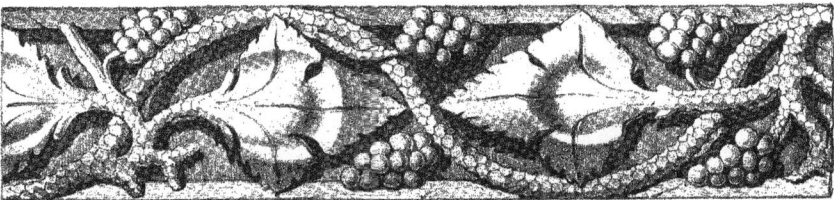

The people in the commercials look too good.
Not like the faces at Walmart. Not like the sad
wanderers on Main Street. Maybe we should
breed icons and have everybody glad.
The people in the commercials look too good.

In heaven, they say, we pick the body we want.
If so, TV is the place to shop. But who will
have the price when whatever's in front
must fit the soul of everything we do.
The people in the commercials look too good.

The poets just keep coming; you have their word.
Applaud them all. For they are able to see
beyond the market where platitudes are heard.
Their metaphors engage the mystery.
The poets just keep coming; you have their word.

So bring them on. We cannot have too many.
They are a sacred choir whose voices grow strong
when truth is clouded. They teach us how to be.
And if you despair, they fill your world with song.
The poets just keep coming; you have their word.

The things that come to you are all you know.
Words are confetti in the wind. And yet
the wind itself, an irresistible flow,
is commanding you and everything you get.
The things that come to you are all you know.

Therefore empty. Embrace your ignorance.
The world has it own fierce scenario.
What you call knowledge is just another trance.
Walk lightly then wherever you must go.
The things that come to you are all you know.

THERE CAN BE NO FAITH
without its shadow, doubt.
The world crowds in and shouts,
"I'm all that is!"
Count the things you cannot
do without.
The highest Truth
fades to nothingness.
There can be no faith without its shadow, doubt.

So live with this polarity. Give your sense
its due when sense makes sense. Yet convene
the holy city in all its magnificence
when the soul confesses to what cannot be seen.
There can be no faith without its shadow, doubt.

The world is full of talk. So many words!
Horizons of testimony. Limitless voices,
like cards in a casino. But no need to curse
the losses. Endless are the chattering choices.
The world is full of talk. So many words.

Wander in any library and get lost
in that wilderness of print. Who does not
witness to this or that? And little cost
to add your own opinion to the lot.
The world is full of talk. So many words.

We are figments in God's imagination.
And the precious perfection of his artistry.
My body, my mind subsist only in
that manifold and are not merely me.
We are figments in God's imagination.

This is the crux of my eternity.
All's known and cherished. Yet out of time,
unalterable, beyond contingency.
This poem's forever then, although not mine.
We are figments in God's imagination.

The world I see has nothing that I want.
It has the flavor of a one-night stand.
Blow a kiss. Yet know this truth up front.
It will not last. It drifts away like sand.
The world I see has nothing that I want.

It is a meal that does not satisfy.
It is the toy under the Christmas tree
that outlives its promise. There is no supply
of beatitude this side of eternity.
The world I see has nothing that I want.

We give the children what they cannot learn,
what innocence already understands.
Not in our rules and stories do they discern
the Truth. They are in creation's hands.
We give the children what they cannot learn.

There is another gospel. See how it shines
in their eyes. That is their Sunday school.
We are but prompters in the play, the lines
set down by an Author we cannot overrule.
We give the children what they cannot learn.

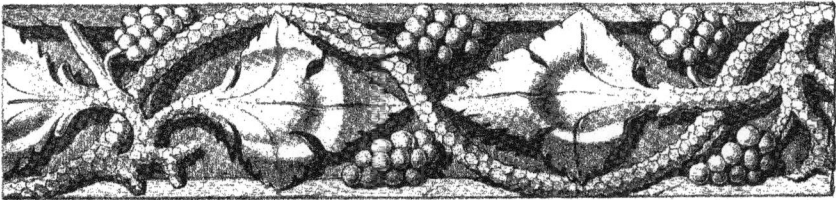

There can be no such thing as pure chance.
Always there is order too. And to this end,
intelligence. And behind intelligence, the dance
of intention. Only a person can intend.
There can be no such thing as pure chance.

The rolling die has a six-sided face.
And a hand does all the casting. Then say not,
"Good Luck!" in parting. Say, "May God's grace
comfort you, and may wisdom be your lot."
There can be no such thing as pure chance.

Too much palaver confounds the gospel.
Though bellowing evangelists may preserve
what already lurks in the heart — God's well-
spring — the sermon of silence will better serve.
Too much palaver confounds the gospel.

Reason unlocks the proverbial narrow gate.
But whosoever would salve the sins of
living must lift himself beyond debate.
In the end, all that persuades is love.
Too much palaver confounds the gospel.

YOU CAN SEE I work
inside the box
juggling rhymes and
fashioning refrains.
In this tight space
ingenuity concocts
ribbons of thought
to justify my pains.
You can see I work inside the box.

Each is a gift waiting beneath your tree.
Untie the knots, and be open to surprise.
Maybe it shows you another way to be.
Maybe it speaks to your innermost surmise.
You can see I work inside the box.

There is laughter at the heart of things.
Whoever that man who has no mind may be,
he jars the hymns with a laugh that brings
hell itself into our solemn liturgy.
There is laughter at the heart of things.

Does he mock our reverence? Or does God remind
that all our piety is chaff? And in a trice
we may become mindless, may be struck blind.
There can be no salvation until we realize
there is laughter at the heart of things.

This love the singers sing of, sweetens the heart.
Who's the fool? The one at the wall who feigns
indifference, holds back? Or the one whose part
quickens his feet, though the dance-music be strange.
This love the singers sing of, sweetens the heart.

Accept the invitation. Arms expand
and gather you in. From bitterness turn
away. It's devotion's waltz. Grand
in its sweep, where epiphanies burn.
This love the singers sing of, sweetens the heart.

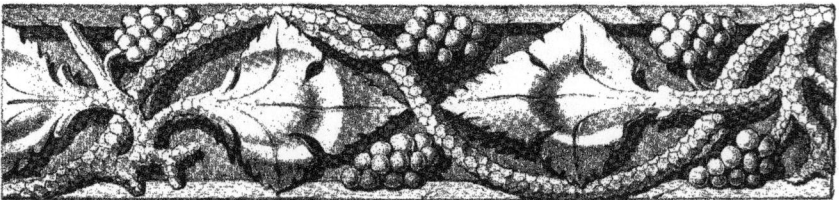

Whatever does God make of all this god-talk?
A piffle? Smoke drifting out of reach?
He cannot be flattered, of course. We walk
in so much ignorance. Simpletons each.
Whatever does God make of all this god-talk?

Words becloud us. All presumptuous thought.
How can a mote engage the sun's essence?
Light alone knows what light has wrought.
And light at last will deliver us to silence.
Whatever does God make of all this god-talk?

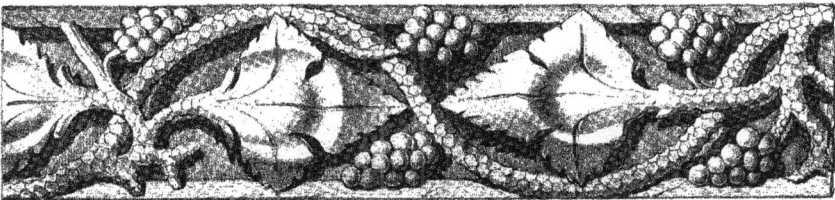

To be a man of faith in a time of doubt
is a strange privilege. When so many refuse
the banquet of grace and elect to live without,
it seems almost weakness to embrace good news,
to be a man of faith in a time of doubt.

Yet I cherish this queer endowment,
taking care how my life is spent.
From the words of the master I discover my bent
and in his company I stand content
to be man of faith in a time of doubt.

There is a light I bring to the world of things.
They become alive. And I see through
them to an omnipresent sun, whose shinings
kindle sight. My vision's then made true.
There is a light I bring to the world of things.

And if I stop to scan a simple leaf,
a universe unfolds in those tiny veins.
And even more: a Face beyond belief!
The One who lives in everything and reigns.
There is a light I bring to the world of things.

You think you have a bone to pick with God.
Don't like the way he runs the world. The lion
should lie down with the lamb. You think it odd
that evil thrives, a scandal, babies are crying.
You think you have a bone to pick with God.

How many worlds have you put together?
What kind of splintered barnyard is your own life?
Wait until pieces mend and chickens gather
before you nag like some annoying wife.
You think you have a bone to pick with God.

Though in the end our bodies betray us all,
keep the faith. To flesh we owe only rent.
Even as hands may shake and syllables crawl
from halting lips, do not grow despondent.
Though in the end our bodies betray us all.

But soaring spirit may thrive in any prison,
even as the blood grows thin and movements lag.
The Christ within can rise beyond all reason
and make of us a triumph. So fly this flag!
Though in the end our bodies betray us all.

You cannot know what you will not know.
Weave the skein of reason how you will.
To arrive at truth, you first must wish to go.
Without inclination the mind is still.
You cannot know what you will not know.

What do you find there in the sky at night?
Your heart whispers, but how do you set your clock?
Do you choose the darkness? Or choose the light?
God honors your wish. Tick tock. Tick tock.
You cannot know what you will not know.

THERE IS A MOMENT
   to join the heretics
and be a Jesus to conventionality.
Let tight-lipped gossips prate.
   Like ticks
they feed on those who
   need their liberty.
There is a moment to join the heretics.

The soul has a Left Bank where iconoclasts
hang out. They dynamite history's debris.
Out of that wreckage, the future is recast
and restless spirit finds new energy.
There is a moment to join the heretics.

We make our way only by degrees.
Here is the lecher still celebrating lust.
And there the monk with his austerities.
Each finds his own purchase as he must.
We make our way only by degrees.

With each grade the world reconstitutes:
the inner attainment transforms the real.
Thus, we cannot appraise the saint's pursuits
until we too become what his acts reveal.
We make our way only by degrees.

There is a throne within that is never empty.
If not God who sits there, an idol will convene
its counterfeit. And it will preside and be
your master. In all things it will intervene.
There is a throne within that is never empty.

Do not suppose that you can demur and live
without a higher purpose. There are imposters
waiting to usurp that seat. Therefore, give
full attention to what your intention serves.
There is a throne within that is never empty.

These poems I lay at the Creator's feet,
orphaned though they may be in the buzz of
the world. Thus do I answer him and repeat
a timeless ſtory out of simple love.
These poems I lay at the Creator's feet,

Not to be be loſt in watery expanses,
where all who need a voice caſt their net
of words. So many ephemeral trances.
But He will not absent Himself. Or forget.
These poems I lay at the Creator's feet,

There is an invisible harvest we are reaping.
The scythes of attention go snickity snack.
In the lofts of our mind, grain is heaping.
When winter comes, we will never lack.
There is an invisible harvest we are reaping.

What you have learned I too shall learn.
Our bushels fill up, a consummation fated.
Only with such bounty can we burn
with what our husbandry's created.
There is an invisible harvest we are reaping.

Do you ever remember how you made that promise
in pre-eternity, before the world was made,
and you consented to be human? A kiss
you gave. And a vow to come to Jesus' aid.
Do you ever remember how you made that promise?

So long ago, but God does not forget.
He dubbed you a knight in the service of the good.
Since you are bound to that etiquette,
be exemplary. Do everything you should.
Do you ever remember how you made that promise?

Stay your hand — evil can't be hidden!
The secret will out. The gallery sees all.
And you will but strike at yourself. For in
this most damnable act we both will fall.
Stay your hand — evil can't be hidden!

Better to be victim than to take this curse
to the grave. Will ever it be erased? The soul
outlasts the world's brief harm. But the worse
fate is yours, who may never again be whole.
Stay your hand — evil can't be hidden!

WE TAKE OUR TURNS
and leap into the dark.
My mother asleep with cancer
on her couch.
My brother in his coffin,
speechless and stark.
My father lying
in a helpless crouch.
We take our turns and leap into the dark.

And you and I will join them. But there is time.
Let us be like diving boys on a cliff bent
over a lake. Staring into the water. Sublime
with the daring and the show of strength,
we take our turns and leap into the dark.

How beautifully they arrive in our world!
Little Devon, with his adventurous eyes.
Lily, dropped from eternity's arms, now curled
in ours, each tiny smile a fond surprise.
How beautifully they arrive in our world!

In their perfection we have our heritage.
And though futures be unknown, they give us
our purpose. For in this generous parentage
hides the One whose handiwork we bless.
How beautifully they arrive in our world!

I am no longer the boy from under the trees.
I stand in the light of a setting sun. My life,
a shadow behind me, with all its memories.
Ahead, mortality with its end to strife.
I am no longer the boy from under the trees.

Strange how it all collapses and comes to be
a single tear, lit up in consciousness,
whether of sorrow or of ecstasy,
a sober mix of regret and thankfulness.
I am no longer the boy from under the trees.

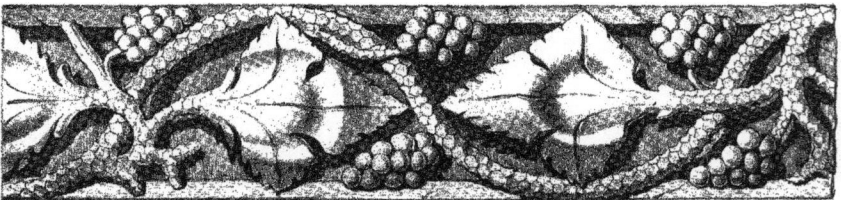

Coming among us, make eternity your gift.
Show the shining face behind your face.
Discover eloquence to make our spirits lift.
Do luminous deeds in this darkened place.
Coming among us, make eternity your gift.

Then we will grasp your hand and confirm
the promise of that solemn covenant,
wherein our quotidian intentions turn
to purest light, and heaven to earth is bent.
Coming among us, make eternity your gift.

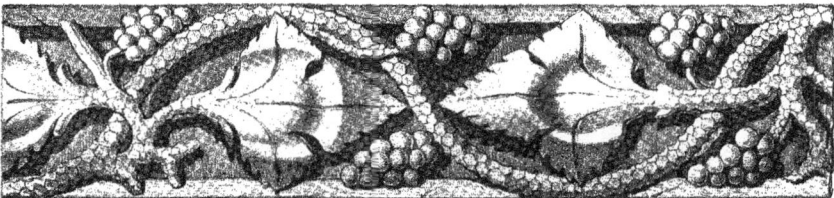

What is there left to do but kneel and pray?
And hope that higher wisdom will prevail.
Predatory armies head this way.
Neither ordinance nor ordnance can avail.
What is there left to do but kneel and pray?

Every dispensation has an end.
The jackals feed upon the fallen deer.
Unless the holy spirit can descend,
apocalypse will find us waiting here.
What is there left to do but kneel and pray?

Yes I am nothing. But nothing can be apart.
For contained in everything, we all become
one. And love itself makes of the heart
a single integer, more than a sum.
Yes I am nothing. But nothing can be apart.

There is no subtraction when God looks down.
I am his darling even when I shrink away,
when I meet his benevolence with a frown
and stain with my darkness his endless day.
Yes I am nothing. But nothing can be apart.

You will remain whatever you've become
in spirit. Even beyond the door of death.
Stand before the mirror. Add up the sum
of what you've chosen, chosen with every breath.
You will remain whatever you've become.

Do not think some last regret will hide
that face. Or rather the face behind that face.
And the very consciousness that waits inside
will shine as your world in that other place.
You will remain whatever you've become.

Ask me what I've come to. This is it.
Something to show for my eighty years.
True or false, this is my best. I pit
myself against forgetfulness and tears.
Ask me what I've come to. This is it.

I do not stand voiceless and noncommittal,
who have words enough for every wild weather.
And if a truth should rise up, after all,
well, your truth and mine will dance together,
Ask me what I've come to. This is it.

Let's hope somehow to be together again.
Maybe we're friends now. While pages turned,
I felt your presence. It grows close when
I think of you and everything we've learned.
Let's hope somehow to be together again.

All this talk was for our good. We go
as one. The veil lifts, and kindred souls
come home. But first these words, which show
us our birthright, the beckoning goal of goals.
Let's hope somehow to be together again.

Seventeen hundred eighty lines is not enough!
Worlds keep coming and the appetite
for life. Death can only be a silly bluff
when all is movement and golden sunlight.
Seventeen hundred eighty lines is not enough!

At every adventure a poem gathers near,
waiting to speak, maybe in my voice.
With such abundance there is nothing to fear.
So do not hush me when I would rejoice.
Seventeen hundred eighty lines is not enough!

ABOUT THE POEMS

These poems are a kind of testimony. When younger, I sought spiritual knowledge in books. Later, the Sufis taught me it resides in the human heart. But most importantly, throughout my life, I was blessed with intimations that could turn into poems. A prayer bead is a reminder. A prayer bead has the power to summon an inspiration, but makes no pretense to comprising it. Poems that approach the ineffable can also serve as pointers. Nothing to quarrel over, just a finger in the moon's direction. In the case of God, the finger must point everywhere.

I am a little astonished that the exacting ten-line form these poems have taken could be so accommodating. They are all round, like prayer beads, the refrain making a perfect circle. How I managed to close the circle so many times, can only be explained as God's will. In time when so few people are capable of faith, I like to think I have been commandeered for a necessary service.

Some of the poems allude to personal allegiances. The "Pir" is the leader of a Sufi order. Sufism has been my mystical education, laid out in the writings of Rumi and Hazrat Inayat Khan. The Sufis teach that all religions point to the same divine Truth. So I also enjoyed an absolute religious freedom. And in my eighties I was able to reprise the Christian church of my boyhood.

On my death bed, I will take pleasure in the thought these poems can go on talking to people in my absence.

INDEX OF FIRST LINES

ABOUT THE POET

Born in 1932, the height of the Depression, Don was the oldest son of Albert and Sylvia Washburn. Albert, a careful, dependable man, worked for the Lehigh Valley Railroad most of his life. Sylvia, a feisty redhead,was a stay-at-home mother. Don and his younger brother Ken attended school in their home town of Easton, Pennsylvania, an ethnically mixed, blue-collar city on the Delaware river. Don's first collection of poems — *The Boy From Under the Trees* — explores that world and the excitement of being able to run free in the neighborhoods for whole summers at a time.

A football scholarship to Yale opened the way to his career as a teacher, first in secondary school. Later, with a Ph.D. in communication from Denver University, he spent over fifty years in college English departments, teaching an enormous variety of subjects, including literature, speech, semantics, and metaphysics. Retired now, since 1971 he had been a professor at the Massachusetts College of Liberal Arts and has made his home in North Adams at the northern edge of the Berkshires. His favorite courses were "The Power of Words," "Science and Spirit," "Rumi's Vision," and "Divine Witness."

During that same period Don, a pliable Geminian, was blessed with five wives (successive, not simultaneous) and four exceptional children, a prodigality shared by many in his generation. Relationships with women have always been an important part of his education and continue to this day to lighten up his life. Of course, love is always a risk, one Don has usually been willing to take. The events, however, depicted in his sonnet cycle, *In The Eye of the Red-Tailed Hawk*, have left him somewhat chastened. Even, so, four of his ex-wives are still dear friends — no small achievement. His children and grandchildren, thanks to their mothers, have turned out to be especially gifted in countless ways.

Don has always been a listener of music, mostly classical, but he had never learned an instrument. With the advent of the computer, he discovered that musical illiteracy was no handicap. With the help of Joseph Schillinger's books and several courses with local composers, he taught himself to make music using the Cakewalk Sonar programs, which are the musical equivalent of word processors. Several pieces that have continued to satisfy him are available on his web site, www.donwashburn.com.

In 1980, Don found his way to the Sufi community at New Lebanon, New York, where he began his spiritual studies in the Sufi Order of the West, led then by Pir Vilayat Khan. The Abode of the Message was his home for two years, and he became not only an initiate, but also a *cherag*, someone trained to preside at Universal Worship Services. He also was a member of the first graduating class of the Suluk Academy, then a four-year program in Sufi studies. The Sufi experience was invaluable in opening his heart to the reality of God. He has also become a communicant in the United Church of Christ. *Prayer Beads* is the harvest taken from these years. The 179 poems are a record of the "wisdom" that the poet, as a perennial seeker, contrives to make his own.

The poet observes, "My life has been showered with blessings, so many that it serves to demonstrate how grace trumps error and shortsightedness. Praise be to the One whose mercy makes everything possible."

ABOUT THIS BOOK

The body type of this book is set in 14-point Adobe Jensen, an oldstyle serif font designed by Robert Slimbach. The Roman face is based on a font cut by Venetian printer Nicolas Jenson around 1470. Since many oldstyle fonts did not incorporate italics, those for this font are based on a set created around 1520 by Ludovico Vincentino degli Arrighi.

The small titles of this book are set in Morris Golden, a font created by William Morris for the Kelmscott Press in 1890. This modern digital recreation of the type by the P22 Type Foundry simulates the soft-edged impression of hand-set metal type on hand-made paper. Morris in turn based his designs on typefaces created by Nicolas Jenson. Larger titles are set in Solemnis, an uncial-style font designed by Günter Gerhard Lange in 1953. Lange created many classic revival fonts for the Berthold foundry, leading that organization through the eras of metal, photo and then digital type design.

The book has been decorated with historic printers' initials and details of Gothic architectural borders to honor and evoke the tradition of the illuminated monk's manuscript.

9780922558834